How to Cut Costs and Expenses in a Business

Effective Cost Reduction Strategies in a Small Business

By Meir Liraz

I0462860

Published by BizMove
www.bizmove.com

ISBN: 9781090402646

Table of Contents

MEIR LIRAZ

1. Introduction

Increasing profits through cost reduction must be based on the concept of an organized, planned program. Unless adequate records are maintained through a proper accounting system, there can be no basis for ascertaining and analyzing costs.

Cost reduction is not simply attempting to slash any and all expenses unmethodically. The owner-manager must understand the nature of expenses and how expenses inter-relate with sales, inventories, cost of goods sold, gross profits, and net profits.

Cost reduction does not mean only the reduction of specific expenses. You can achieve greater profits through more efficient use of the expense dollar. Some of the ways you do this are by increasing the average sale per customer, by effectively using display space and thereby increasing sales volume per square foot, by getting a larger return for your advertising and sales promotion dollar, and by improving your internal methods and procedures.

Profit is in danger when good merchandising and cost control do not go hand in hand. A big sales volume does not necessarily mean a big profit, as one retailer, Carl Jones, learned.

Jones's pride was stocking stylish and well assorted lines of merchandise. Each year, sales volume increased. This increase was attributed to good merchandise which Jones felt took care of the steady rise in expenses.

But Mr. Jones began to have doubts when he found it necessary to get bank loans more often than had been his practice. When he discussed the problem with his banker, Jones was advised to check expenses. As the banker said, "A large and increasing sales volume often creates the appearance of prosperity while behind-the-scene expenses are eating up the profit."

2. Paying The Right Price

Your goal should be to pay the right price for prosperity. Determining that price for your operation goes beyond knowing what your expenses are. Reducing expenses to increase profit requires you to obtain the most efficient use of the expense dollar.

Look, for example, at the payroll expense. Salesclerks are paid to sell goods, and their productivity is the key to reducing the payroll cost.

If you train a salesclerk to make multiple sales at higher unit prices, you increase productivity and your profits without adding dollars to your payroll expenses. Or, if four salesclerks can be trained to sell the amount previously sold by seven, the payroll can be cut by three persons.

An understanding of the worth of each expense item comes from experience and an analysis of records. Adequate records tell what has happened. Their analysis provide facts which can help you set realistic goals, you are paying the right price for your store's prosperity.

3. Analyzing Your Expenses

Sometimes you cannot cut an increase item. But you can get more from it and thus increase your profits. In analyzing your expenses, you should use percentages rather than actual dollar amounts.

For example, if you increase sales and keep the dollar amount of an expense the same, you have decreased that expense as a percentage of sales. When you decrease your cost percentage, you increase your percentage of profit.

On the other hand, if your sales volume remains the same, you can increase the percentage of profit by reducing a specific item of expense. Your goal, of course, is to do both: to decrease specific expenses and increase their productive worth at the same time.

Before you can determine whether cutting expenses will increase profits, you need information about your operation. This information can be obtained only if you have an adequate recordkeeping system. Such records will provide the figures to prepare a profit and loss statement (preferably monthly for most retail businesses), a budget, break-even calculations, and evaluations of your operating ratios compared with those of similar types of business.

4. Break-Even Analysis

A useful method for making expense comparisons is break-even analysis. Break-even is the point at which gross profit equals expenses. In a business year, it is the time at which your sales volume has become sufficient to enable your over-all operation to start showing a profit. The two condensed profit and loss statements, in the accompanying example, illustrate the point. In statement "A", the sales volume is at the break-even point and no profit is made. In statement "B" for the same store, the sales volume is beyond the break-even point and a profit is shown. In two statements, the percentage factors are the same except for fixed expenses, total expenses, and operating profit.

	A		B	
	Break-Even Amount	Percent of sales	Profit Amount	Percent of sales
Sales	500,000	100	600,000	100
Cost of Sales	300,000	60	360,000	60
Gross Profit	200,000	40	240,000	40
Operating Expenses				
Fixed	150,000	30	150,000	25
Variable	50,000	10	60,000	10
Total	200,000	40	210,000	35
Operating Profit	$ NONE	0	30,000	5

As shown in the example, once your sales volume reached the break-even point, your fixed expenses are covered. Beyond the break-even point, every dollar of sales should earn you an equivalent additional profit percentage.

It is important to remember that once sales pass the break-even point, the fixed expenses percentage goes down as the sales volume goes up. Also the operating profit percentage increases at the same rate as the percentage rate for fixed expenses decreases - provided, of course, that variable expenses are kept in line. In the illustration, fixed expenses in Statement "B" decreased by 5 percent and operating profit increased by 5 percent.

5. Locating Reducible Expenses

Your profit and loss (or income) statement provides a summary of expense information and is the focal point in locating expenses that can be cut. Therefore, the information should be as current as possible. As a report of what has already been spent, a P and L statement alerts you to expense items that bear watching in the present business period. If you get a P and L statement only at the end of the year, you should consider having one prepared more often. At the end of each quarter might be often enough for some firms. Ideally, you can get the most recent information from a monthly P and L.

Regardless of the frequency, for the most information two P and L statements should be prepared. One statement should report the sales, expenses, profits and/or loss of your operations cumulatively for the current business year to date. The other should report on the same items for the last complete month or quarter. Each of the statements should also carry the following information:

(1) this year's figures and each item as a percentage

of sales.

(2) last year's figures and the percentages.

(3) the difference between last year and this year - over or under.

(4) budgeted figures and the respective percentages.

(5) the difference between this year and the budgeted figures - over and under.

(6) average percentages for your line of business (industry operating ratio) when available, and

(7) the difference between your annual percentages and the industry ratios - under or over.

This information allows you to locate expense variation in three ways: (1) by comparing this year to last year, (2) by comparing expenses to your own budgeted figures, and (3) by comparing your percentages to the operating ratios for your line of business. The important basis for comparison is the percentage figure. It represents a common denominator for all three methods. When you have indicated the percentage variations, you should then study the dollar amounts to determine what line of operative action is needed.

Because your cost cutting will come largely form variable expenses, you should make sure that they are flagged on your P and L statements. Variable expenses are those which fluctuate with the increase or decrease of sales volume. Some of them are: advertising, delivery, wrapping supplies, sales salaries, commissions, and payroll taxes. Fixed expenses are those which stay the same regardless of sales volume. Among them are: your salary, salaries for permanent non-selling employees (for example, the bookkeeper), depreciation, rent, and utilities.

6. Taking Action

When you have located a problem expense area, the next step obviously is to reduce that cost so as to increase your profit. A key to the effectiveness of your cost-cutting action is the worth of the various expenditures. As long as you know the worth of your expenditures, you can profit by making small improvements in expenses. Keep an open eye and an open mind. It is better to do a spot analysis once a month than to wait several months and then do a detailed study. Take action as soon as possible. You can refine your cost-cutting action as you go along.

Bonus Guide

7. Introduction to Financial Management

Financial management in the small firm is characterized, in many different cases, by the need to confront a somewhat different set of problems and opportunities than those confronted by a large corporation. One immediate and obvious difference is that a majority of smaller firms do not normally have the opportunity to publicly sell issues of stocks or bonds in order to raise funds. The owner-manager of a smaller firm must rely primarily on trade credit, bank financing, lease financing, and personal equity to finance the business. One, therefore faces a much more severely restricted set of financing alternatives than those faced by the financial vice president or treasurer of a large corporation.

On the other hand, many financial problems facing the small firm are very similar to those of larger corporations. For example, the analysis required for a long-term investment decision such as the purchase of heavy machinery or the evaluation of lease-buy alternatives, is essentially the same regardless of the size of the firm. Once the decision is made, the financing alternatives available to the firm may be radically different, but the decision process will be generally similar.

One area of particular concern for the smaller business owner lies in the effective management of working capital. Net working capital is defined as the difference between current assets and current liabilities and is often thought of as the "circulating capital" of the business. Lack of control in this crucial area is a primary cause of business failure in both small and large firms.

The business manager must continually be alert to changes in working capital accounts, the cause of these changes and the implications of these changes for the financial health of the company. One convenient and effective method to highlight the key managerial requirements in this area is to view working capital in terms of its major components:

(1) Cash and Equivalents

This most liquid form of current assets, cash and cash equivalents (usually marketable securities or short-term certificate of deposit) requires constant supervision. A well planned and maintained cash budgeting system is essential to answer key questions such as: Is the cash level adequate to meet current expenses as they come due? What are the timing relationships between cash inflows and outflows? When will peak cash needs occur? What will be the magnitude of bank borrowing required to meet any cash shortfalls? When will this borrowing be necessary and when may repayment be expected?

(2) Accounts Receivable

Almost all businesses are required to extend credit to their customers. Key issues in this area include: Is the amount of accounts receivable reasonable in relation to sales? On the average, how rapidly are accounts receivable being collected? Which customers are "slow payers?" What action should be taken to speed collections where needed?

(3) Inventories

Inventories often make up 50 percent or more of a firm's current assets and therefore, are deserving of close scrutiny. Key questions which must be considered in this area include: Is the level of inventory reasonable in relation to sales and the operating characteristics of the business? How rapidly is inventory turned over in relation to other companies in the same industry? Is any capital invested in dead or slow moving stock? Are sales being lost due to inadequate inventory levels? If appropriate, what action should be taken to increase or decrease inventory?

(4) Accounts Payable and Trade Notes Payable

In a business, trade credit often provides a major source of financing for the firm. Key issues to investigate in this category include: Is the amount of money owed to suppliers reasonable in relation to purchases? Is the firm's payment policy such that it will enhance or detract from the firm's credit rating? If available, are discounts being taken? What are the timing relationships between payments on accounts payable and collection on accounts receivable?

(5) Notes Payable

Notes payable to banks or other lenders are a second major source of financing for the business. Important questions in this class include: What is the amount of bank borrowing employed? Is this debt amount reasonable in relation to the equity financing of the firm? When will principal and interest payments fall due? Will funds be available to meet these payments on time?

(6) Accrued Expenses and Taxes Payable

Accrued expenses and taxes payable represent obligations of the firm as of the date of balance sheet preparation. Accrued expenses represent such items as salaries payable, interest payable on bank notes, insurance premiums payable, and similar items. Of primary concern in this area, particularly with regard to taxes payable, is the magnitude, timing, and availability of funds for payment. Careful planning is required to insure that these obligations are met on time.

As a final note, it is important to recognize that although the working capital accounts above are listed separately, they must also be viewed in total and from the point of view of their relationship to one another: What is the overall trend in net working capital? Is this a healthy trend? Which individual accounts are responsible for the trend? How does the firm's working capital position relate to similar sized firms in the industry? What can be done to correct the trend, if necessary?

Of course, the questions posed are much easier to ask than to answer and there are few "general" answers to the issues raised. The guides which follow provide suggestions, techniques, and guidelines for successful management which, when tempered with the experience of the individual owner-manager and the unique requirements of the particular industry, may be expected to enhance one's ability to manage effectively the financial resources of a business enterprise.

MEIR LIRAZ

MEIR LIRAZ

www.ingramcontent.com/pod-product-compliance
Lightning Source LLC
Chambersburg PA
CBHW072311170526
45158CB00003BA/1285